# COZY QUILTS

## A Charming Blend of Wool Appliqué and Cotton Patchwork

···❦ By Tara Lynn Darr ❧···

# COZY QUILTS

**A Charming Blend of Wool Appliqué and Cotton Patchwork**

By Tara Lynn Darr

**Editor:** Kimber Mitchell
**Designer:** Bob Deck
**Photography:** Aaron T. Leimkuehler
**Illustration:** Lon Eric Craven
**Technical Editor:** Deanna Hodson
**Photo Editor:** Jo Ann Groves

**Published by:**
Kansas City Star Books
1729 Grand Blvd.
Kansas City, Missouri, USA 64108

First edition, first printing
ISBN: 978-1-61169-095-8

Library of Congress Control Number: 2013939159

Printed in the United States of America by Walsworth Publishing Co., Marceline, MO

To order copies, call StarInfo at (816) 234-4242.

# TABLE OF CONTENTS

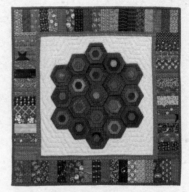

# ABOUT THE AUTHOR

Tara Lynn Darr comes from a long line of quilters. Growing up in a tiny town in Indiana, she often visited family members who quilted and sewed. As an adult, she turned her love of sewing into a cottage industry, making dolls and other creations from her home and then selling them at craft fairs. Eventually, she moved to Joliet, Illinois, where she currently resides with her husband, two children, and a lovable family basset hound.

Tara's passion for quilting was sparked in 1999, when a friend invited her to attend an international quilt show. Since then, quilting and crafting have opened many doors of opportunity. She now designs her own patterns through her Sew Unique Creations pattern company. Tara's designs have also been published in *American Patchwork & Quilting* magazine and in *Simply Charming: Small Scrap Quilts of Yesteryear*, her first book with Kansas City Star Quilts. She also wrote a book on rug hooking and has self-published two of her own quilting books.

You can find Tara at many of the national quilting shows, selling fabrics, notions, and patterns that have tickled her fancy. When she's not traveling to quilt shows, blogging, Facebooking, or playing in a pile of fabric, she enjoys creating quilts inspired by the past, hand-piecing quilts, reading, cooking, visiting family members, and riding her four-wheeler down dirt roads and trails.

For more information on Tara's designs, visit her website at **www.sewuniquecreations.com**, her blog at **www.sewuniquecreations.blogspot.com**, or her Facebook page where she enjoys the lively banter of her many quilting friends. Find her on Facebook by entering her business name, Sew Unique Creations, in the search box.

Someday, Tara hopes to enjoy a slow-paced life in the Appalachian Mountains surrounded by its beautiful scenery while operating a destination quilt shop on her property. She also dreams of finishing and publishing the witty quilting novel she is currently writing.

# ACKNOWLEDGMENTS

Thanks to each and every person in my life who has encouraged me to continue doing what I love to do.

To my husband and children for allowing me to take over the house with everything quilting-related and for your patience, kindness, love, and support.

To Kimber Mitchell, my editor and fellow quilt lover. You made the process of writing a book simple and easy. You are a treasure to the quilt world and myself. I'm so lucky to have you as my editor!

To Aaron Leimkuehler, photographer extraordinaire. What a gem you are! Your eye for photography is lovely. Thank you for taking such great care with my quilts.

To my illustrator, Lon Eric Craven, for your artistic skills in creating this book's helpful diagrams.

To my book designer genius, Bob Deck. Your creative skills amaze me. Thank you for bringing this book to life with but a few scraps of fabric.

To Deanna Hodson, my technical editor, for double-checking the accuracy of my instructions.

And last but not least, Doug Weaver for giving me this wonderful opportunity to write a second book for Kansas City Star Quilts.

# DEDICATION

*Thank you to each of the wonderful quilters in my family. You have all helped me grow as a quilter while inspiring me to do the things in life that I love most. I hope to pass this quilting legacy on to my own family so it can live on for generations to come.*

# INTRODUCTION

My love affair with wool began several years ago when I met a sweet lady named Debbie through an online crafting forum. Although we became friends, we never had the chance to meet in person before she passed away from breast cancer. I still think of her often and am grateful to her for sharing her knowledge of wool, penny rugs, and rug hooking with me. She was a kind, gentle soul.

My passion for all things wool grew over the years, and I can satisfy all my creative passions between wool projects, quilting, and rug hooking! Wool adds such a warm texture and feel to a variety of projects, plus it's so easy to work with. It reminds me of the warm friendships that grow from teaching others how to use this wonderful fiber.

My wool stash is overflowing but never complete. I'm constantly on the hunt for just the right color and will never have enough wool in my stash—just as we quilters will never have enough fabric in our stashes! While searching for wool, I often find gorgeous antique pieces in perfect condition tucked into a corner of the antique stores that I haunt. In fact, old Army blankets and I have become best friends as I really love that shade of green for my projects. I also often purchase old wool clothing or wool yardage and use it as it is.

Local and online quilt shops are also a great source for wool. I purchase hand-dyed wool from two of my favorite wool vendors, who also happen to be close friends. (You can find them and vendors who sell wool by the yard in our resource section on pages 79 and 80.) Hand-dyed wool can also be found on Ebay and Etsy. In addition to buying wool, I occasionally hand-dye a bit of my own. The art of hand-dyeing wool is a fun process, but you must use caution when working with the chemicals necessary to achieve gorgeous colors.

Scrappy quilts and little quilts have always been a passion of mine. Mixing wonderful wools and cotton prints, I combined those two loves in this book, and you have in your hands the result of a quilter gone wild and still running with scissors. Sorry, Mom, for breaking that rule!

I hope the 11 small wool-on-cotton quilts that I have created for you will bring you as much joy, warmth, and happiness as they did me!
Happy Stitching!

# WOOL APPLIQUÉ BASICS

I love working with wool because it is such an easy and forgiving fabric and lends a beautiful texture to my projects. If you are new to this wonderful fiber, you are in for a treat. Once wool has been felted, the edges will not fray, so there is no need to turn under the edges of your appliqué pieces as you might do for traditional cotton appliqué. In this section, I've gathered all the basic tips and tricks for working with wool that I have come to love. To familiarize yourself with this versatile fiber, I also encourage you to take a class on wool appliqué at your local quilt shop. Wool sewing bees where you can enhance each other's stashes by sharing bits and pieces of wool are also a fun creative outlet.

## FELTING WOOL

Use felted wool for your stitching projects. The hand-dyed wool at quilt shops and quilt shows is typically already felted, but ask if in doubt. Wool purchased off the bolt will need to be felted. To do this, simply submerge the wool in very hot water with a small amount of soap, if desired, and agitate it. This process will shrink the wool fibers, melding them together so they won't ravel. For larger pieces, use your washer for this task. For small pieces, you can use your kitchen or bathroom sink. Allow the wool to soak in the hot water for a few minutes, then gently squeeze out the water, and dry the wool in a hot dryer. (Do not use fabric softener.) Properly felted wool will have no or minimal fraying on its edges. If you have a particularly loose-woven wool that won't felt well, use a fusible web product to prevent fraying when you appliqué it. Another option to prevent raveling is to apply Fray Check to the wool edges. It will dry clear but it leaves the edges of the wool a bit stiff, and it will wash away if you ever wash your finished project.

## NEEDLES

I use a size #24 chenille needle for 90% of my wool work. The other sizes feel too thick in my hand. For best results, test out different needle sizes to see which one feels most comfortable to you. Chenille needles are very sharp, which help them easily slide through layers of wool and fusible web. Plus, they have a larger eye, which better accommodates thicker threads that are often used on wool projects. I prefer Richard Hemming chenille needles or the chenille needles sold exclusively at Primitive Gatherings Quilt Shop in Menasha, Wisconsin, because they glide through wool effortlessly and have a superb finish with no burrs that snag fibers. When I'm stitching thick vine shapes or using two strands of No. 12 Perle cotton in different colors twisted to make fancy letters or leaf veins, I switch to a size #22 chenille needle because its eye is even bigger and more easily accommodates the thicker thread.

## THREAD

I like to use a few different types of thread when appliquéing wool:

### Valdani Perle Cotton Size 12 (100% Hand-Dyed and Colorfast)

I love this thread and used its size 12 for all the projects in this book. I primarily used black (#893), but also sprinkled some other colors throughout the projects. The twelve colors I used in this book, which are also available as a boxed set from Valdani, are: O 511 (antique black/brown), 0 196 (light brown), H207 (blue), H205 (tan), O86 (purple), 893 (antique black), O510 (orange), O519 (green), O78 (deep red), O540 (green/black), P5 (gold), and H204 (deep pink). These threads have subtle color changes throughout them, which adds a wonderful effect to the projects.

### Wool Floss

This floss is a dream to work with and adds a great finished look to wool projects. Wool thread tends to stretch or fray after being passed through the wool fabric over time, which can result in twisted threads. To prevent this, I recommend using shorter lengths of thread on your needle.

### Other Options

I also like to use two or three strands of Valdani hand-dyed embroidery floss, Week's Dye Works embroidery floss, and The Gentle Art thread.

## SCISSORS

I like to use very sharp scissors with a short blade because my cutting is more precise on small- and medium-sized pieces. For large pieces, I typically switch to a bit longer-bladed scissors IF the pieces do not require a lot of intricate or detailed cutting.

## TEMPLATES

First and foremost, when tracing pattern shapes for wool appliqué, trace directly on the pattern lines given—not to the right or left of them! I have seen many quilters cut their shapes too small or too large because of imprecise tracing. If the template lines are thick, trace the templates in the center of those lines— unless the pattern asks you do to otherwise. To trace templates, I recommend using a mechanical pencil or fine-point Sharpie marker. If using one of these, you should not be able to see your drawn lines after cutting out your templates. If you are stitching a project with several circles in it, I recommend purchasing a handy circle template at your local office supply store (usually located in the drafting supply aisle) or quilt shop. I like to use a green plastic template set that contains several circle sizes, each labeled with their specific size. Circle templates also come in clear plastic.

## APPLIQUÉ PREPARATION

To accurately position my appliqué pieces, I first find the center of the background fabric by folding it in half diagonally and vertically, then finger-pressing it. If your background fabric is light or medium colored, a light box works wonderfully for positioning the appliqué. Place your pattern sheet on top of the light box, right side up, then your background fabric, right side up, on top of that. I prefer to use fusible web because the pieces will lightly stick to the background fabric, allowing you to more easily transfer the fabrics to your ironing board without them shifting. Using the pattern sheet as a guide, position the appliqué pieces and iron them in place if using fusible web, or glue them if using the Freezer-Paper method.

For dark fabrics, use a pattern overlay created with a sheet of thick, clear plastic used to cover picnic tables. This is typically sold by the yard. For smaller projects, quilter's template plastic works well. You can also use interfacing or any sheer, transparent fabric. Begin by marking the center of the overlay with horizontal, vertical, and if necessary, diagonal lines. Then trace the design onto the overlay. Lay your background fabric, right side up, on your pressing station, then place the pattern overlay on top and begin arranging the appliqué shapes underneath the overlay. A pair of tweezers can help in placing tiny pieces. When you're satisfied with the arrangement, remove the pattern overlay and press the appliqué in place with a steam iron if using fusible web.

## WOOL APPLIQUÉ METHODS

Two of the most common techniques for wool appliqué use fusible web or freezer paper.

**Fusible Web Method**

For my wool appliqué projects, I love to use Steam-A-Seam 2 fusible web because it creates smooth, neat appliqué shapes. Fusible web is particularly helpful when using a loosely-woven wool because it will help prevent the wool from stretching out of shape when appliquéing it. It will also help prevent your wool shapes from shifting around on the background fabric as you stitch them down. When using Steam-A-Seam 2, one side is used to trace the design and the other protects the sticky side that will be adhered to the wool. The latter side will be the least sticky and is easier to remove the paper liner from. Before I trace anything, I peel back a bit of the paper to reveal the fusible web so I can figure out which side to trace my templates on.

1. Cut a piece of the Steam-A-Seam 2 a little larger than the shape you want to trace.

2. Trace the shapes on the side of the paper liner that wants to stick to the fusible web, and remove the second liner of paper. Trace the shapes about ½" apart from each other on the remaining paper lining. If shapes will use different color wools, cut them out ¼" outside the drawn lines. If not, then leave them as is as shown in the following diagram.

3. Apply the Steam-A-Seam 2 to the wrong side of the wool. (Wool typically does not have a wrong or right side, but with hand-dyed wools, where mottling can vary from front to back, it is a good idea to check which side you prefer before adhering the Steam-A-Seam 2.)

4. Cut out the shapes directly on the drawn lines.

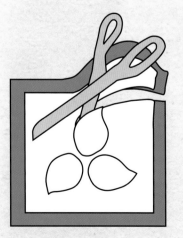

5. Allow the wool to cool, then peel off the remaining paper liner.

6. Press the wool to the cotton fabric for 10-15 seconds, using a bit of steam from your iron and moving it constantly to avoid unsightly iron marks on your wool. Repeat for the remaining wool shapes.

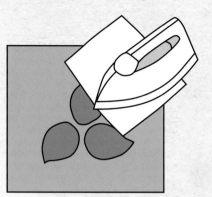

7. Flip your project over and press again from the wrong side of the project.

If you use this appliqué method, you will need to reverse the templates for the Summer Garden, Prairie Rose Patch, and Full Bloom projects in this book. To reverse the templates, simply make a copy of them, place the copy on a light box or tape it with the wrong side facing you onto a window, then tape an additional sheet of paper over the template and trace the shapes onto that paper. Some printers can also reverse patterns.

### Freezer Paper Method

Freezer paper has a dull side as well as shiny side that temporarily adheres to fabric when pressed with a warm iron, making it handy for cutting wool appliqué templates. Trace the templates onto the dull side of the paper, leaving about ¼"–½" of space between each of the traced shapes. Roughly cut out the templates (there is no need to cut them out perfectly on the traced line), then position them on your selected wools. Iron the freezer-paper templates to the wools with the shiny side down, using the wool setting on your iron. The templates will adhere to the wool temporarily. You can peel off the paper and reposition the templates if necessary, and you can reuse the freezer-paper templates a few more times before you have to discard them. To secure the wool appliqué pieces to the background fabric, I use Roxanne's Glue Baste-It. It only takes a small dot of glue to hold them in place.

If using the Freezer Paper method, you do not need to reverse the templates for the Summer Garden, Prairie Rose Patch, and Full Bloom projects in this book.

## APPLIQUÉING MULTIPLE LAYERS

When appliquéing more than one layer of wool pieces, work from top to bottom. For example, if a design features a flower center on top of a flower, stitch the flower center to the flower BEFORE stitching the flower to the background fabric. Stitching through all layers at once can be bulky and cumbersome. To reduce bulk when appliquéing multiple layers with fusible web, I cut out the middle of some of the fusible web pieces, leaving about ¼" of it inside the drawn line. This technique is often referred to as the "Donut" method.

**Throughout this section, I have mentioned various products that I like to work with. I am fortunate to have several local shops where I can purchase them. If you can't find these supplies in your area, see our resource guide on page 79 for mail-order sources that can help you.**

# MIDNIGHT TWINKLE

## Designed and made by Tara Lynn Darr

•••⁘❦⟶ Finished size: 15" x 18½" ⟵❦⁘•••

*A star-studded array of assorted wool scraps twinkles against a single dark background fabric in this charming little quilt.*

## FABRIC REQUIREMENTS

○ 20—4" squares of assorted color wool scraps for stars

○ 16" x 20" black cotton print for background

○ 21" x 25" fabric of choice for backing

○ ¼ yard black cotton print for binding

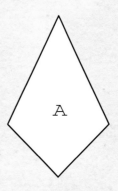

TEMPLATE

## CUTTING INSTRUCTIONS

From assorted color wool squares, cut:
• 80 of Template A to the right

From black print, cut:
• 2—2½" strips the width of fabric for binding

### TARA'S TIPS

To make this quilt even scrappier, use several different wool scraps instead of the suggested 20 in the instructions. If you want an exceptionally scrappy look, why not use 80 different fabrics for the star segments? Don't be picky with your colors—use a little of everything! Even the ugliest fabrics are beautiful when they are cut small enough!

# SEWING INSTRUCTIONS

1. Using a chalk pencil or a removable fabric marking pen, draw a 14" x 17½" rectangle on the black print background fabric. This will provide a basic guideline to follow when arranging your wool star segments later.

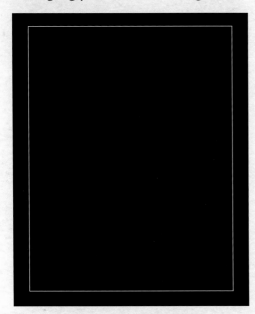

2. Using a ruler and a marking pencil or pen, lightly draw a 3½" square in the upper left-hand corner of the drawn 14" x 17½" rectangle, using the previously drawn rectangle as a guide.

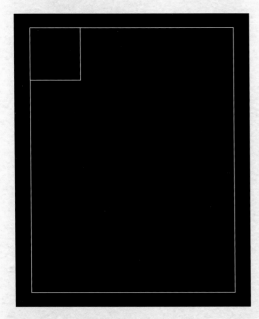

3. Using a ruler and a marking pencil or pen, lightly draw a vertical and horizontal line that divides the previously drawn 3½" square into four equal 1¾" squares. These drawn lines will provide a basic guideline to follow when arranging your wool star segments in the following step.

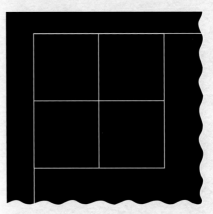

4. Using the previously drawn lines as a guide, lay out four of the wool star segments on the black background fabric, leaving about ¹⁄₁₆" of space between them so that the threads will lay nice and flat when appliquéing the star segments later. Each of the outer points should touch the outer drawn lines of the 3½" square.

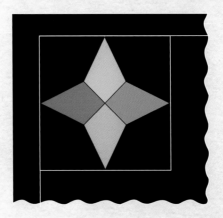

5. Continue adding stars to the black background until you have 20 of them. Tara found it easy to do this without marking additional lines by simply following the larger 14" x 17½" drawn line. However, if you find it difficult to position the wool stars, simply continue drawing the necessary number of 3½" squares separated into four equal quadrants as described in the previous steps.

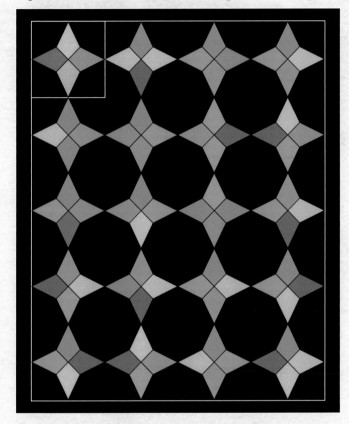

6. When satisfied with the placement of all stars, affix them by pressing if using fusible, glue baste, or pin if not. This will keep them in place as you sew. Using a blanket stitch, appliqué the star segments to the black print background.

## Blanket Stitch

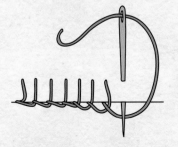

7. Following the manufacturer's instructions for removing the pencil or pen markings, remove all the drawn lines.

8. Trim the quilt to measure 15" x 18½", leaving ½" around all the outer edges of the stars.

9. Sandwich the quilt top, batting, and backing; baste. Quilt as desired, then bind. Tara hand-quilted her project, using matching quilting thread and the Big Stitch method (a form of hand quilting done with a larger stitch and Perle cotton, regular hand-quilting thread, or crochet thread). She outline-stitched around each star, which creates a nice octagon shape.

# THIS 'N THAT

Designed and made by Tara Lynn Darr

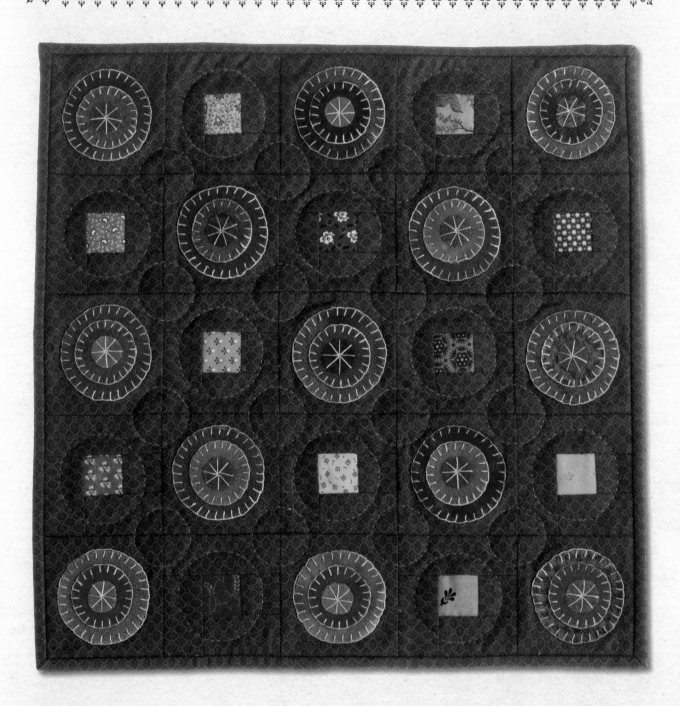

Finished size: 15½" x 15½"

*I enjoyed piecing the stacked wool circles in this quilt and watching their layers of color create wonderful eye candy. Blanket-stitching adds a simple yet striking embellishment to their edges. Made of cotton scraps, the alternating framed square blocks are a charming companion to the circle blocks and sew up quickly.*

## FABRIC REQUIREMENTS

○ 13—5" squares of assorted color wools for circle blocks

○ 12—1½" squares of assorted color cotton prints for framed square blocks

○ ⅝ yard brown print for background and binding

○ 21" square fabric of choice for backing

## CUTTING INSTRUCTIONS

From assorted color wool squares, cut:
❧ 13 of Template A on page 24 for large circles (or you can use a 2¼"-diameter plastic circle template)
❧ 13 of Template B on page 24 for medium circles (or you can use a 1½"-diameter plastic circle template)
❧ 13 of Template C on page 24 for small circles (or you can use a ¾"-diameter plastic circle template)

From brown print, cut:
❧ 13—4" squares for wool appliqué blocks
❧ 12—1½" squares for framed square blocks
❧ 24—1½" x 2½" rectangles for framed square blocks
❧ 12—1½" x 3½" rectangles for framed square blocks
❧ 2—2½" strips the width of fabric for binding

From assorted color cotton prints, cut:
❧ 12—1½" squares for framed square blocks

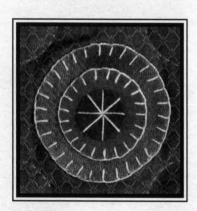

# SEWING INSTRUCTIONS

## Circle Blocks

1. Layer a large, medium, and small circle on top of a 4" brown print square.

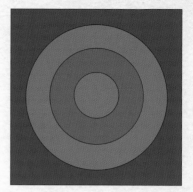

2. Affix in place by pressing if using fusible, glue baste, or pin if not. This will keep them in position as you sew. Using a blanket stitch, sew around the perimeter of each of the circles. Note that the small top circle features very long stitches that meet in the center.

3. Repeat steps 1 and 2 to create a total of 13—4" squares with layered circles. Trim each of the squares to measure 3½" square. (The blocks are cut larger originally to accommodate the distortion that can occur during the appliqué process.)

## Framed Square Blocks

1. Sew one 1½" brown print square to a colored print 1½" square. Press the seam toward the brown print.

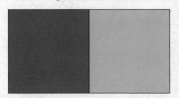

2. Sew one 1½" x 2½" brown print rectangle to the top of the unit from the previous step. Press the seam toward the brown print.

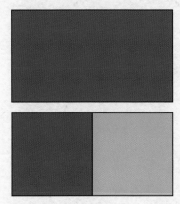

3. Sew one 1½" x 2½" brown print rectangle to the right side of the unit from the previous step. Press the seam toward the brown print.

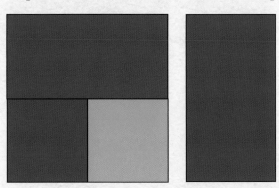

4. Sew one 1½" x 3½" brown print rectangle to the bottom of the unit from the previous step. Press the seam toward the brown print. This completes the block, which should measure 3½" square.

5. Repeat steps 1–4 to create a total of 12 framed square blocks.

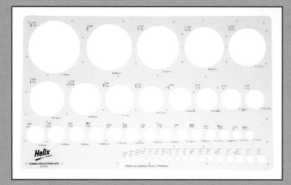

When working with projects that have several circle shapes in it, consider purchasing a set of circle templates (available at office supply stores and quilt shops). They're worth every penny. I have a green plastic set that even includes the outer vertical and horizontal center markings on the outside of each circle. These markings come in handy when arranging your circles on the background fabric and especially when working with patterned wools such as herringbone, houndstooth, or plaid.

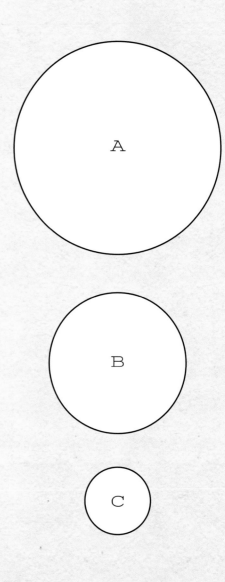

TEMPLATES

## Quilt Assembly

1. Referring to the quilt assembly diagram below, lay out the 13 circle blocks and 12 framed square blocks. Sew the blocks into five rows, then join the rows to complete the quilt top, which should measure 15½" square.

2. Sandwich the quilt top, batting, and backing; baste. Quilt as desired, then bind. Tara hand-quilted her project with a matching light tan thread, using the Big Stitch method (a form of hand quilting done with a larger stitch and Perle cotton, regular hand-quilting thread, or crochet thread). She stitched a large 2½" circle around each of the small 1" center squares on the cotton fabric blocks, then quilted small 1½" circles centered over the seams where the blocks meet.

QUILT ASSEMBLY DIAGRAM

# SUMMER GARDEN

Designed and made by Tara Lynn Darr

⚜ Finished size: 15" x 19½" ⚜

*I love my summer garden and all its flowers that bloom with an exuberance of color. I created this little quilt to brighten my day during the winter months when I cannot enjoy my garden flowers.*

## FABRIC REQUIREMENTS

- 12—2½" squares of assorted color wools for flowers

- 12—1½" squares of assorted color wools for flower centers

- 8" square green wool for stems and leaves

- 12—4½" squares of assorted cream or light tan cotton prints for block backgrounds

- 20—1½" squares of assorted cream or light tan cotton prints for sashing

- 31—1½" x 4" assorted medium/dark cotton prints for sashing

- 21" x 26" fabric of choice for backing

- ¼ yard brown print for binding

## CUTTING INSTRUCTIONS

*If using the fusible web appliqué method, you will need to reverse the templates. For instructions on how to reverse templates, see page 14 in the **Wool Appliqué Basics** section.*

From 2½" assorted color wool squares, cut:
- 12 of Template A below for flowers

From 1½" assorted color wool squares, cut:
- 12 of Template B below for flower centers (or you can use a ⅞"-diameter plastic circle template)

From green wool, cut:
- 12 of Template C below for stems

- 12 of Template D below for leaves

From brown print, cut:
- 2—2½" strips the width of fabric for binding

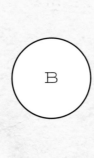
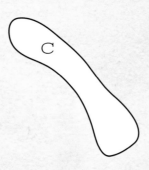

TEMPLATES

# SEWING INSTRUCTIONS

1. Referring to the following diagram for placement, position the flower, flower center, stem, and leaf on the 4½" cream/tan print square.

2. When satisfied with placement, affix in place by pressing if using fusible, glue baste or pin if not. This will keep them in position as you sew. Using a blanket stitch, appliqué each of the shapes to each of the 4½" cream/tan print squares.

3. Repeat steps 1 and 2 to create a total of 12—4½" wool flower blocks. Then trim each of the blocks to measure 4" square. (The blocks are cut larger originally to accommodate the distortion that can occur during the appliqué process.)

4. Referring to the quilt assembly diagram on page 29, lay out the 12 flower blocks, 20—1½" cream/light tan print squares, and the 31—1½" x 4" rectangles. Sew the units into nine rows, then join the rows to complete the quilt top.

5. Sandwich the quilt top, batting, and backing; baste. Quilt as desired, then bind. Tara quilted her project using the Big Stitch method (a form of hand quilting done with a larger stitch and Perle cotton, regular hand-quilting thread, or crochet thread). She quilted straight lines through the sashing squares and rectangles to make the flower blocks pop out more.

QUILT ASSEMBLY DIAGRAM

# PETALS ON PARADE

Designed and made by Tara Lynn Darr

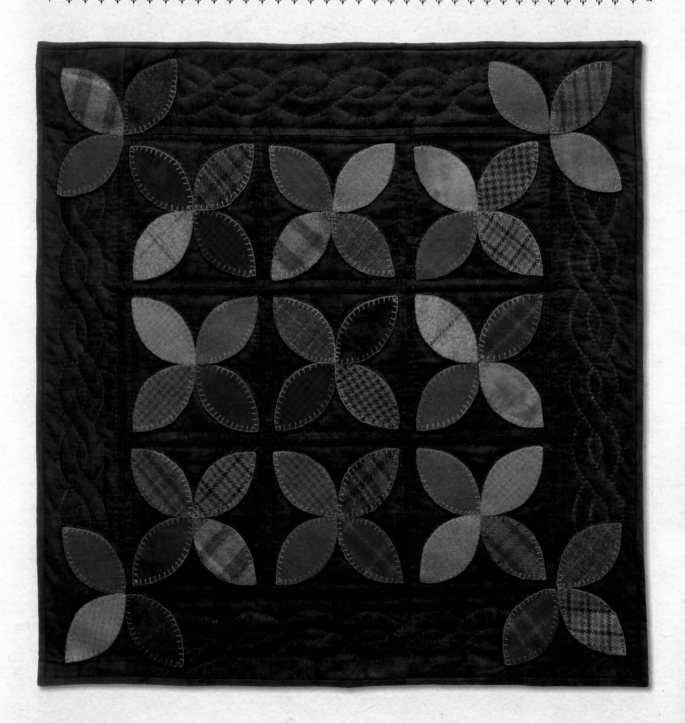

Finished size: 25½" x 25½"

*A cozy medley of wool melon shapes takes center stage against a mottled black cotton background in this quilt that exudes a warm, old-fashioned flair.*

## FABRIC REQUIREMENTS

○ 48—2¼" x 4" assorted color wools for melons

○ 1⅛ yards mottled black cotton fabric for block backgrounds, border, and binding

○ 32" square fabric of choice for backing

## CUTTING INSTRUCTIONS

From assorted color wools, cut:
❧ 48 of Template A below

From mottled black cotton, cut:
❧ 9—7" squares for block backgrounds
❧ 2—4" x 18½" strips for side borders
❧ 2—4" x 25½" strips for top and bottom borders
❧ 3—2½" strips the width of fabric for binding

## TARA'S TIPS

I love blanket-stitching my wool appliqué with Valdani's hand-dyed, black mottled Perle cotton thread. I typically use size 12 thread because it is thin enough to add that extra pop of color and definition to the finished projects without looking too thick or chunky. For this project, I used a gorgeous size 12 Valdani tan color (#O196). I love the antique effect it adds to the finished piece.

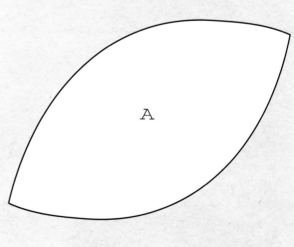

A

TEMPLATE

# SEWING INSTRUCTIONS

1. To find the exact center of a 7" black print square, fold it in half vertically and finger-press, then fold it in half horizontally and finger-press. Referring to the following diagram for placement, lay out four wool melons so they almost meet in the center of the black square, leaving about ¹⁄₁₆" of space in the center for the thread to lay nice and flat when appliquéing the melons later.

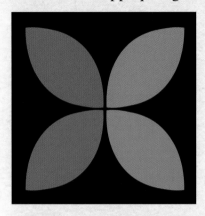

2. When satisfied with placement, affix in place by pressing if using fusible, glue baste or pin if not. This will keep them in position as you sew. Using a blanket stitch, appliqué the wool melons to the black print squares.

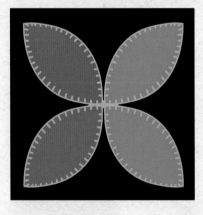

3. Repeat steps 1 and 2 to create a total of 9–7" square blocks (the remaining 12 melons will be used in the border later). Trim each of the blocks to measure 6½" square. (The blocks are cut larger originally to accommodate the distortion that can occur during the appliqué process.)

4. Referring to the quilt assembly diagram on page 33, lay out the 9–6½" blocks. Sew them into three rows of three blocks each, then join the rows to create the quilt center.

5. Referring to the quilt assembly diagram, sew the 2–4" x 18½" border strips to the sides of the quilt center.

6. Referring to the quilt assembly diagram, sew the 2–4" x 25½" border strips to the top and bottom of the quilt top.

7. Referring to the photo of the quilt on page 30 for placement, lay out three melons in each of the border's four corners so that each of the points nearly touch each other. When satisfied with placement, affix in place by pressing if using fusible, glue baste or pin if not. This will keep them in position as you sew. Using a blanket stitch, appliqué the melons to the border.

## Blanket Stitch

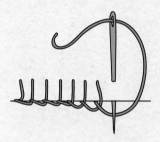

8. Sandwich the quilt top, batting, and backing; baste. Quilt as desired, then bind. Tara hand-quilted about ⅛" away from each of the melon shapes to make them pop against the cotton background blocks. In the border, she hand-quilted a 2"-wide cable design, using an EZ Mark stencil (see Resources on page 80 for contact information).

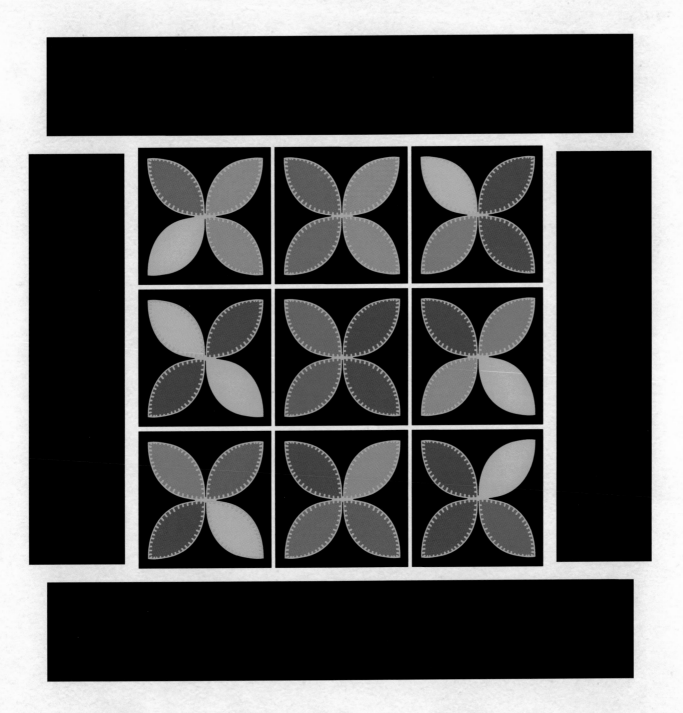

QUILT ASSEMBLY DIAGRAM

# TIMELESS HEXAGONS

Designed and made by Tara Lynn Darr

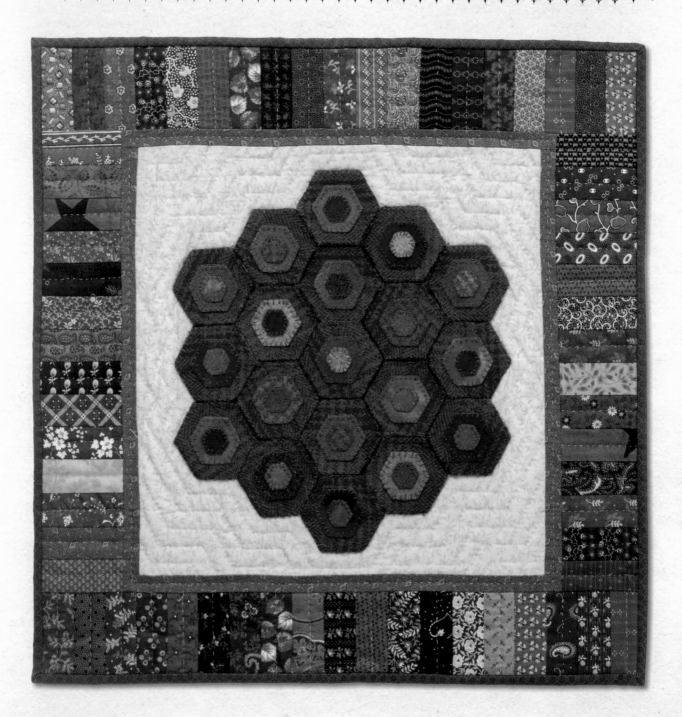

◆◦◦◦⟡ Finished size: 19½" x 19½" ⟡◦◦◦◆

*I love hexagon shapes and have made several quilts with them. For this project, I drew three different sized hexagons and stacked them to create a layered effect. Use small scraps of wool to create the quilt center design and cotton scraps for the outer border.*

## FABRIC REQUIREMENTS

- ○ 14" square brown plaid wool for large hexagons

- ○ 19—2" squares of assorted color wools for medium hexagons

- ○ 19—1½" squares of assorted color wools for small hexagons

- ○ 33—4" squares of assorted color cotton prints for outer border

- ○ ½ yard light tan cotton print for background

- ○ ⅛ yard brown cotton print for inner border

- ○ 26" square fabric of choice for backing

- ○ ¼ yard dark brown cotton print for binding

## CUTTING INSTRUCTIONS

From brown plaid wool, cut:
- ❧ 19 of Template A below for large hexagons

From 2" assorted color wool squares, cut:
- ❧ 19 of Template B below for medium hexagons

From 1½" assorted color wool squares, cut:
- ❧ 19 of Template C below for small hexagons

From light tan print, cut:
- ❧ 1—14½" square for background

From brown print, cut:
- ❧ 2—1" x 13½" strips for inner side borders
- ❧ 2—1" x 14½" strips for inner top and bottom borders

From *each* of the 4" assorted color print squares, cut:
- ❧ 2—1½" x 3" rectangles for outer border

From dark brown print, cut:
- ❧ 3—2½" strips the width of fabric for binding

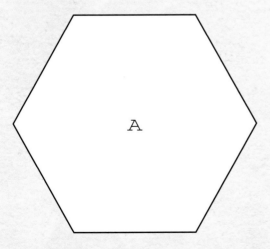

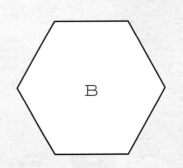

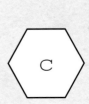

A

B

C

TEMPLATES

# SEWING INSTRUCTIONS

## Quilt Center

1. Fold the 14½" light tan print square in half vertically and finger-press. Open the fabric up and fold it in half horizontally and finger-press. Position one brown plaid wool hexagon in the center of the light tan print square, using the horizontal fold line as a guide for the hexagon's left and right edges and the vertical line as a guide for the hexagon's top and bottom edge.

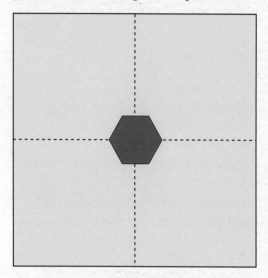

2. Arrange six brown plaid wool hexagons around the center hexagon from the previous step, leaving about ⅟₁₆" of space between the hexagon shapes for the thread to pass through so it lays nice and flat when appliquéing the hexagons later.

3. Arrange the remaining 12 brown plaid hexagons around the unit from the previous step, leaving about ⅟₁₆" of space between the hexagon shapes.

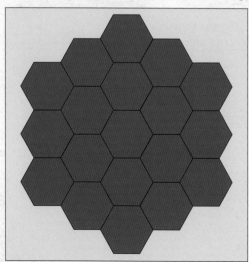

4. When satisfied with placement, affix in place by pressing if using fusible, glue baste or pin if not. This will keep them in position as you sew. Using a blanket stitch, appliqué the brown plaid hexagons to the light tan print background.

Blanket Stitch

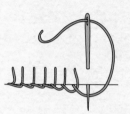

5. Center each of the small hexagons on top of each of the medium hexagons. Affix in place using your chosen method. Using a blanket stitch, appliqué the small hexagons to the medium hexagons.

6. Center the small/medium hexagons from the previous step over the large brown plaid wool hexagons, affix in place using your chosen method, then blanket-stitch them to the large brown plaid wool hexagons.

7. Trim the light tan print square to measure 13½" square.

## TARA'S TIPS

Take your time when arranging the layered hexagons in the quilt center. Remember to leave about $\frac{1}{16}$" of space between the large brown plaid hexagons so that your threads will lay nice and flat instead of bunching up after they're stitched in place. If you can still see a little of the background fabric once you've stitched all the hexagons in place and that bothers you, you can use a fabric marker in the same brown shade as the larger hexagons to disguise the exposed background.

## Inner Border

Referring to the quilt assembly diagram below, sew the 2—1" x 13½" strips to the sides of the quilt center. Then sew the 2—1" x 14½" strips to the top and bottom of the quilt top.

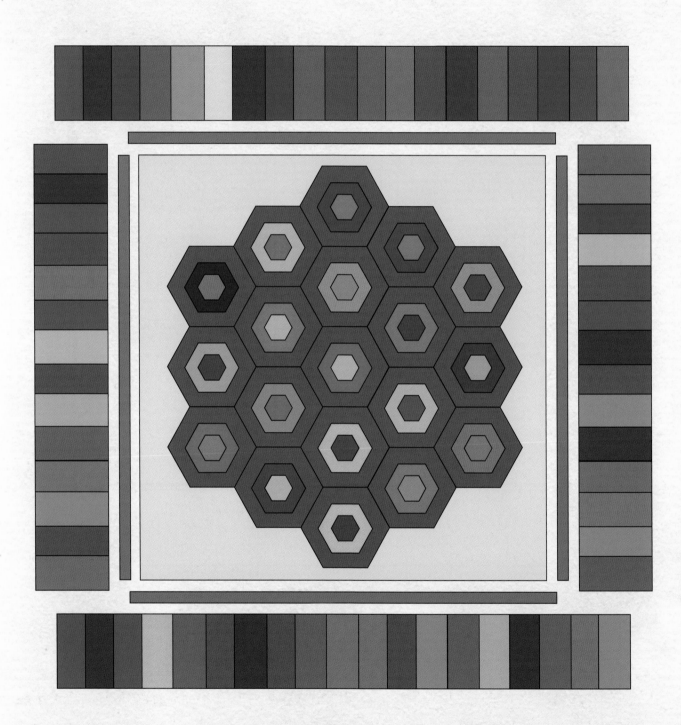

QUILT ASSEMBLY DIAGRAM

## Outer Border

1. Sew together 14—1½" x 3" assorted print rectangles along their long sides to create a side border strip that measures 3" x 14½". Press the seams in the same direction. Repeat to make a second side border strip.

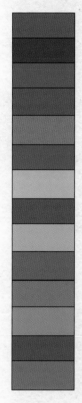

2. Referring to the quilt assembly diagram, sew the two strips from the previous step to the sides of the quilt center. Press the seams toward the inner border.

3. Sew together 19—1½" x 3" rectangles along their long sides to create a top border strip that measures 3" x 19½". Press the seams in the same direction. Repeat to make a bottom border strip.

4. Referring to the quilt assembly diagram, sew the two strips from the previous step to the top and bottom of the quilt top. Press the seams toward the inner border.

5. Sandwich the quilt top, batting, and backing; baste. Quilt as desired, then bind. Using the Big Stitch method (a form of hand quilting done with a larger stitch and Perle cotton, regular hand-quilting thread, or crochet thread) and a light color thread that matches the quilt center's background, Tara quilted ½" away from the large hexagon shape, and outlined the hexagon with rows of quilting spaced ½" apart from the center. She also used the Big Stitch method to quilt straight through the center of the inner border and the center of each of the rectangles in the outer border.

# PRAIRIE ROSE PATCH

Designed and made by Tara Lynn Darr

Finished size: 19½" x 19½"

*I love flowers and often incorporate them into my designs.*
*Eye-popping reds, greens, and golds illuminate a mottled*
*black background in this flowering beauty. To create*
*an eye-catching effect, I stitched the appliqué pieces with*
*black mottled thread.*

## FABRIC REQUIREMENTS

○ 12" square green wool for leaves and stems

○ 4" square red wool for small red flowers

○ 5" square red plaid wool for medium flowers

○ 2" x 7" gold wool for flower accents

○ ⅜ yard red stripe wool for large center flower

○ 4" square light brown plaid wool for flower centers

○ ⅝ yard black cotton print for block background and
   outer border

○ ⅜ yard red cotton stripe for inner border and binding

○ 26" square fabric of choice for backing

# CUTTING INSTRUCTIONS

*If using the fusible web appliqué method, you will need to reverse the templates. For instructions on how to reverse templates, see page 14 in the **Wool Appliqué Basics** section. Labels below correspond to template labels on page 45. Please refer to those before cutting fabrics so you know which piece needs to be cut with what fabric.*

From green wool, cut:
- 4 of Template F on page 45 for stems
- 4 of Template G on page 45 for leaves
- 4 of Template K on page 45 for long stem

From red stripe wool, cut:
- 1 of Template H on page 45 for large center flower

From gold wool, cut:
- 1 of Template I on page 45 for medium center flower
- 4 of Template B on page 45 for flower accents

From light brown plaid wool, cut:
- 1 of Template J on page 45 for center flower's center
- 4 of Template C on page 45 for four corner flower centers
- 4 of Template E on page 45 for flower center

From red plaid wool, cut:
- 4 of Template A on page 45 for four corner flowers

From red wool, cut:
- 4 of Template D on page 45 for flowers

From black print, cut:
- 1—13½" square for block background
- 2—3½" x 13½" strips for side outer borders
- 2—3½" x 19½" strips for top and bottom outer borders

From red stripe, cut:
- 2—1" x 12½" strips for side inner borders
- 2—1" x 13½" strips for top and bottom inner borders
- 3—2½" strips the width of fabric for binding

# SEWING INSTRUCTIONS

**Center Block**

1. Fold the 13½" black print square in half vertically and finger-press. Open the fabric up and fold it in half horizontally, and finger-press. Then finger-press intersecting diagonal lines.

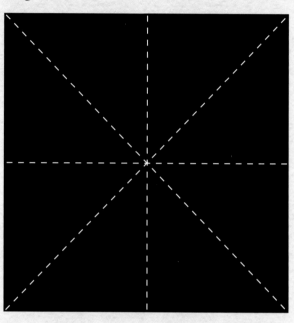

2. Referring to the diagram below and templat on page 45 for placement, lay out the appliq pieces on the black print square, using the finger-pressed lines from the previous step a guide. The dashed lines on the template pag indicate where certain pieces overlap.

3. When satisfied with placement, affix in place by pressing if using fusible, glue baste or pin if not. This will keep them in position as you sew. Using a blanket stitch, appliqué the wool pieces to the background block. Sew short stem stitches through the centers of the large green leaves.

Blanket Stitch

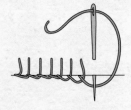

Stem Stitch

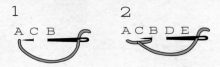

4. Trim the block to measure 12½" square.

## Inner Border

1. Referring to the quilt assembly diagram on page 44, sew 2—1" x 12½" red stripe strips to the sides of the quilt center.

2. Referring to the quilt assembly diagram, sew 2—1" x 13½" red stripe strips to the top and bottom of the quilt top.

## Outer Border

1. Referring to the quilt assembly diagram, sew 2—3½" x 13½" strips to the sides of the quilt center.

2. Referring to the quilt assembly diagram, sew 2—3½" x 19½" strips to the top and bottom of the quilt top.

Sandwich the quilt top, batting, and backing; baste. Quilt as desired, then bind. Tara loves the look of hand-quilted fancy borders, so she used a swag template (#HOL-403-02) from The Stencil Company (see Resources on page 80 for contact information). For the appliqué block, she hand-quilted about ⅛" away from the center wool flower medallion to make each of the wool pieces pop out. She stitched a straight line through the center of the inner border.

QUILT ASSEMBLY DIAGRAM

TEMPLATES

# STAR PLAY

Designed and made by Tara Lynn Darr

Finished size: 18" x 18"

*Six-pointed stars are fun to stitch with scraps of wool.*

*To make my quilt more colorful and playful, I added big*

*circles around the border and in the quilt center. An easy*

*"piano key" border and sashing are quick to make with*

*leftover scraps of cotton fabric.*

## FABRIC REQUIREMENTS

- ○ 12—3½" squares of assorted color wools for stars

- ○ 9—2½" squares of assorted color wools for circles

- ○ ¼ yard cream cotton print for star blocks

- ○ 30—3" squares of assorted medium/dark cotton prints for sashing and borders

- ○ 9—2½" squares of assorted medium/dark cotton prints for sashing and border cornerstones

- ○ 24" square fabric of choice for backing

- ○ ¼ yard black cotton print for binding

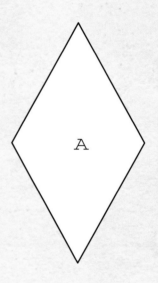

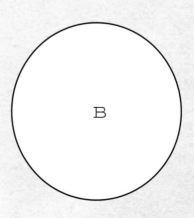

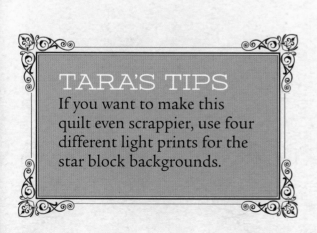

## TARA'S TIPS
If you want to make this quilt even scrappier, use four different light prints for the star block backgrounds.

TEMPLATES

## CUTTING INSTRUCTIONS

From *each* of the 3½" assorted color wool squares, cut:

❧ 2 of Template A on page 47 for a total of 24 star points

From 2½" assorted color wool squares, cut:

❧ 9 of Template B on page 47 for circles (or use a 1⅞" plastic circle template)

From cream print, cut:

❧ 4—6" squares for block backgrounds

From 2½" assorted medium/dark print squares, cut:

❧ 9—2½" squares for sashing and border cornerstones

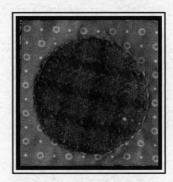

From *each* of the 3" assorted medium/dark print squares, cut:

❧ 2—1½" x 2½" rectangles for a total of 60 sashing and border rectangles

From black print, cut:

❧ 3—2½" strips the width of fabric for binding

# SEWING INSTRUCTIONS

1. Fold a 6" cream print square in half horizontally and finger-press. Open the fabric up and fold it in half vertically, then finger-press.

2. Using the finger-pressed lines from the previous step as a guide, center the six wool star points on the cream print square, leaving about $\frac{1}{16}$" of space between each star point so that the thread can easily pass around each shape and will lay nice and flat when appliquéing the star points later.

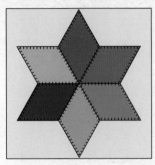

3. When satisfied with placement, affix in place by pressing if using fusible, glue baste or pin if not. This will keep them in position as you sew. Using a blanket stitch, appliqué the wool pieces to the background block.

### Blanket Stitch

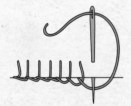

4. Repeat steps 1–3 to create a total of 4—6" wool star blocks. Trim each of the blocks to measure $5\frac{1}{2}$" square. (The blocks are cut larger originally to accommodate the distortion that can occur during the appliqué process.)

5. Center a wool circle over a $2\frac{1}{2}$" colored print square. Affix in place using your chosen method. Using a blanket stitch, appliqué each circle to its background block.

6. Sew together 5—$1\frac{1}{2}$" x $2\frac{1}{2}$" assorted print rectangles along their long sides to create a strip that should measure $2\frac{1}{2}$" x $5\frac{1}{2}$". Press seams in one direction. Repeat to make a total of 12 of these strips for the sashing and border.

7. Referring to the diagram below, lay out the four star blocks, 9—$2\frac{1}{2}$" squares with stitched circles, and 12 sashing and border strips from the previous step into five rows.

**8.** Referring to the quilt assembly diagram below, sew together the units from the previous step to complete the quilt top.

QUILT ASSEMBLY DIAGRAM

9. Sandwich the quilt top, batting, and backing; baste. Quilt as desired, then bind. Tara stitched in-the-ditch around each of the stars and circles. Using the Big Stitch method (a form of hand quilting done with a larger stitch and Perle cotton, regular hand-quilting thread, or crochet thread), she quilted down the center of each of the strips in the "piano key" border and sashing.

# TEXAS STAR

Designed and made by Tara Lynn Darr

Finished size: 20½" x 22½"

*These Texas Star blocks are a breeze to make with scraps of wool. A scrappy sashing and border of cotton prints add pizzazz to this sparkling design.*

## FABRIC REQUIREMENTS

○ 5" square plaid wool for star centers

○ 12—3" x 5" of assorted color wools for star points

○ 1⅜ yards cream cotton print for block, sashing, border backgrounds, and binding

○ 23—5" charm squares or assorted medium/dark cotton prints for sashing and borders

○ 27" x 29" fabric of choice for backing

## CUTTING INSTRUCTIONS

From 5" plaid wool square, cut:
❧ 4 of Template A on page 57 for star centers

From *each* of 12—3" x 5" assorted color wools, cut:
❧ 2 of Template B on page 57 for a total of 24 star points

From cream print, cut:
❧ 4—8½" x 9½" rectangles for blocks
❧ 9—2½" squares for sashing and border cornerstones
❧ 90—1⅞" squares for sashing and border backgrounds
❧ 3—2½" strips the width of fabric for binding

From 5" charm squares or assorted medium/dark prints, cut:
❧ 90—1⅞" squares for sashing and borders

## TARA'S TIPS

If you want to make this quilt even scrappier, use several different light fabrics for the star block and border backgrounds.

# SEWING INSTRUCTIONS

## Star Blocks

1. Fold the 8½" x 9½" cream print rectangle in half horizontally and finger-press. Open the fabric up and fold the rectangle in half vertically and finger-press.

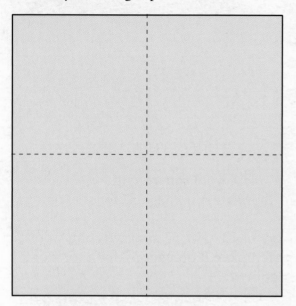

2. Using the finger-pressed lines from the previous step as a guide, center a wool star center on the cream print rectangle.

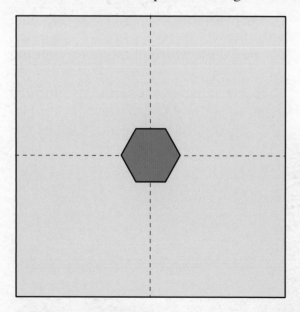

3. Using the finger-pressed lines from step 1 as a guide, position two wool star points above and below the star center, leaving about ¹⁄₁₆" of space between each shape so that the thread will lay nice and flat when appliquéing the pieces later.

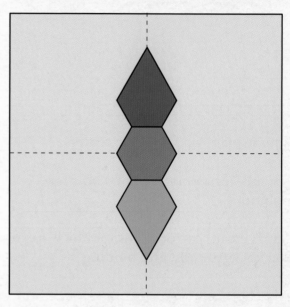

4. Using the finger-pressed lines as a guide, position the remaining four star points on the background block, leaving about ¹⁄₁₆" of space between them.

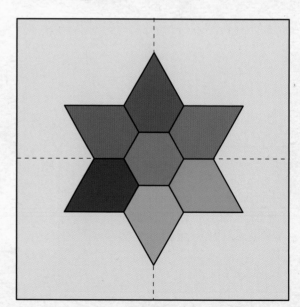

**5.** When satisfied with placement, affix in place by pressing if using fusible, glue baste or pin if not. This will keep them in position as you sew. Using a blanket stitch, appliqué the wool pieces to the background block.

Blanket Stitch

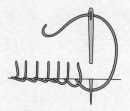

**6.** Repeat steps 1–5 to create a total of 4—8½" x 9½" wool star blocks.

**7.** Trim each of the blocks to measure 7½" x 8½". (The blocks are cut larger originally to accommodate the distortion that can occur during the appliqué process.)

## Sashing and Border

1.  On the wrong side of the 90—1⅞" light print squares, mark a diagonal line from corner to corner with a permanent pen, pencil, or chalk marker.

2.  With right sides together, layer the light print square on top of a dark print square and sew ¼" from both sides of the drawn line.

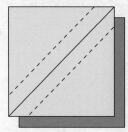

3.  Cut the square apart on the drawn line. You should have two half-square triangle units that measure 1½" square.

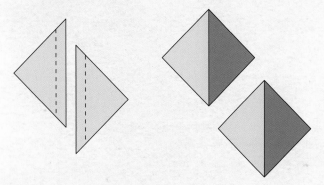

4.  Repeat steps 2 and 3 to create a total of 180 half-square triangle units.

5.  Referring to the following diagram, sew together 14 half-square triangle units into two rows of seven units each. Press seams in opposite directions in each of the rows. Then sew the two rows together and press the seams open. This strip is one of six used in the horizontal rows of the quilt. Repeat to create a total of six of these strips.

**6.** Referring to the following diagram, sew together 16 half-square triangle units into two rows of eight units each. Press seams in opposite directions in each of the rows. Then sew the two rows together and press the seams open. This strip is one of six vertical rows used in the sashing and border. Repeat to create a total of six of these strips.

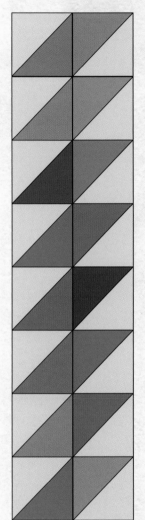

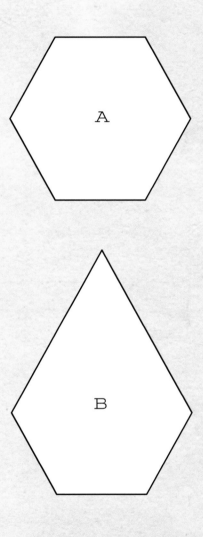

TEMPLATES

## Finishing the Quilt

1.  Referring to the quilt assembly diagram on page 59, lay out the four star blocks, 9—2½" cream print squares, and 12 border and sashing strips from steps 5 and 6 on pages 56 and 57. Sew the units into five rows, then join the rows to complete the quilt top.

2.  Sandwich the quilt top, batting, and backing; baste. Quilt as desired, then bind. Tara stitched in-the-ditch around each of the stars, then outline-quilted ½" away from each star. Using the Big Stitch method (a form of hand quilting done with a larger stitch and Perle cotton, regular hand-quilting thread, or crochet thread), she quilted an X through each of the 2" finished cream print squares in the border and sashing and a line through each of the small cream print sides of the half-square triangle units.

### TARA'S TIPS

Become one with your pins. I know a lot of quilters don't like to use them, but they really come in handy with smaller projects like these, especially when sewing the blocks together so that you get accurate intersections where they meet.

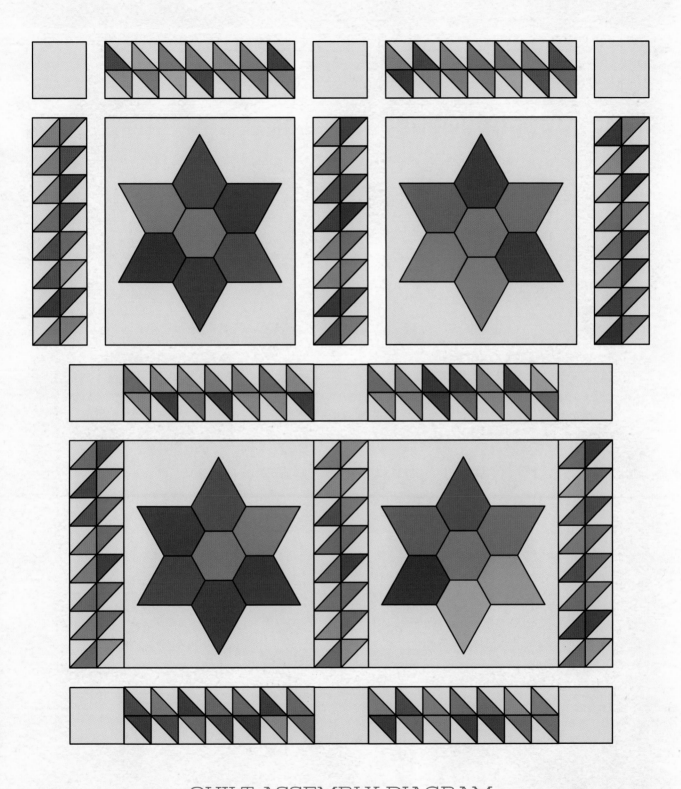

QUILT ASSEMBLY DIAGRAM

# SEVEN SISTERS

Designed and made by Tara Lynn Darr

•••✦❧  Finished size: 17" x 19"  ❧✦•••

*I dream of making a Seven Sisters quilt someday and have started tucking away fabrics for it. In the meantime, I thought I would make a small wool-on-cotton quilt that showcases a single Seven Sisters block. Its multi-colored stars are a great way to use up your wool scraps—or a good excuse to buy wool if you don't have scraps on hand!*

## FABRIC REQUIREMENTS

- ○ 10" x 16" brown plaid wool for large star points

- ○ 14—3" x 4" assorted color wools for small star points

- ○ ¾ yard cream cotton print for background and binding

- ○ 23" x 25" fabric of choice for backing

## CUTTING INSTRUCTIONS

From brown plaid wool, cut:
- ◈ 6 of Template A below for large star points

From *each* of the 3" x 4" assorted color wools, cut:
- ◈ 3 of Template B below for a total of 42 small star points

From cream print, cut:
- ◈ 1—18" x 20" rectangle for background
- ◈ 2—2½" strips the width of fabric for binding

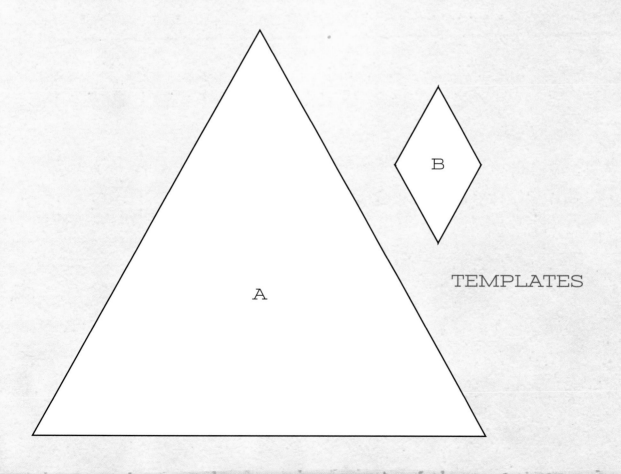

B

A

TEMPLATES

# SEWING INSTRUCTIONS

1.  Fold the 18" x 20" cream print rectangle in half horizontally and finger-press it. Open the fabric up and fold it in half vertically and finger-press it.

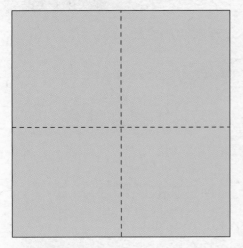

2.  Using the finger-pressed lines from the previous step as a guide, arrange the six star points on the cream print rectangle, leaving about ⅟₁₆" of space between each shape so that the thread can easily pass around each shape and lay nice and flat when appliquéing the star points later.

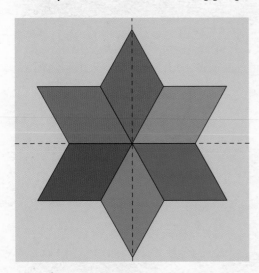

3.  Using the finger-pressed horizontal line from step 1 as a guide, lay out six more star points on each side of the one from the previous step.

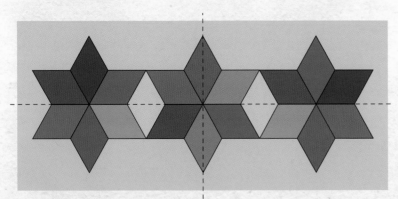

**4.** Using the finger-pressed vertical line from step 1 and previously positioned stars as a guide, lay out two additional stars (12 star points) *above* the stars from the previous step.

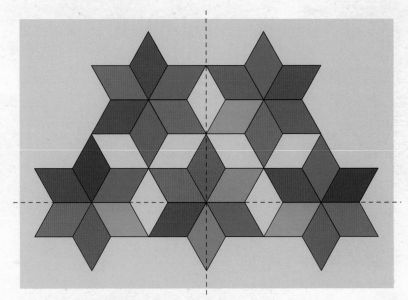

**5.** Using the finger-pressed vertical line from step 1 and previously placed stars as a guide, lay out two additional stars (12 star points) *below* the stars from the previous step.

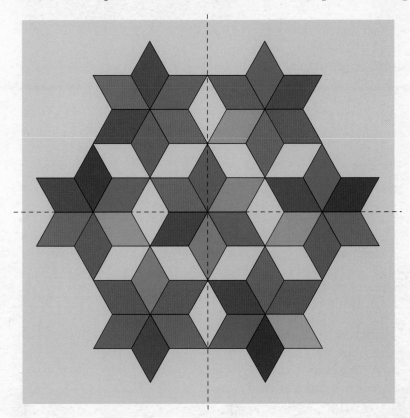

6.  Using the horizontal and vertical finger-pressed lines from step 1 and previously placed stars as a guide, lay out the six large brown plaid wool star points around the seven smaller stars.

7.  When satisfied with placement, affix in place by pressing if using fusible, glue baste or pin if not. This will keep them in position as you sew. Using a blanket stitch, appliqué each of the star points to the background block.

Blanket Stitch

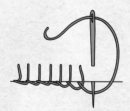

8.  Trim the cream print background rectangle to measure 17" x 19". (The block was cut larger originally to account for the distortion that can occur during the appliqué process.)

9.  Sandwich the quilt top, batting, and backing; baste. Quilt as desired, then bind. Tara stitched in-the-ditch around each of the small stars and each of the large brown plaid wool star points. Using the Big Stitch method (a form of hand quilting done with a larger stitch and Perle cotton, regular hand-quilting thread, or crochet thread), she stitched a diamond grid spaced 1" apart on the background print.

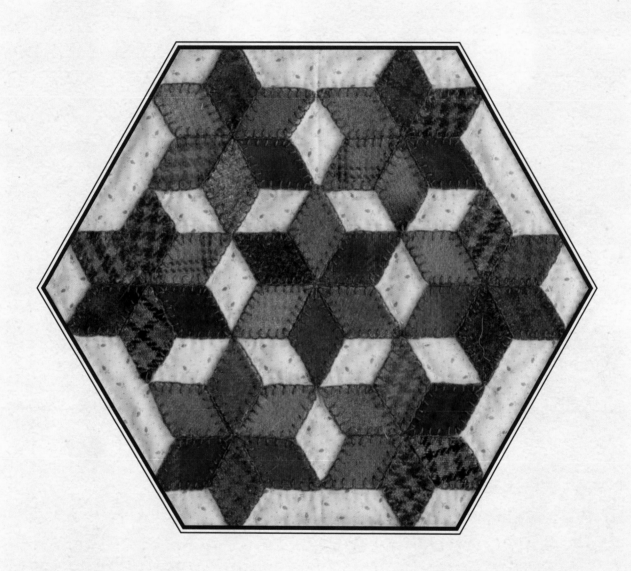

# DELIGHTFUL DRESDENS

Designed and made by Tara Lynn Darr

Finished size: 31" x 31"

*The classic Dresden Plate pattern has long captured quilters' hearts. I made a bed-size quilt in this pattern with cotton fabrics and it's one of my favorite quilts to snuggle under when the weather turns cold. For a fun twist on the Dresden theme, I designed this wool-on-cotton quilt with a muted palette of wools. The result is a timeless charm that makes it look as though it was created years ago.*

## FABRIC REQUIREMENTS

○ 8" square dark mustard plaid wool for Dresden centers

○ 28—5" squares of assorted color wools for Dresden petals

○ 1⅝ yards black cotton print for background and binding

○ 37" square fabric of choice for backing

## CUTTING INSTRUCTIONS

From dark mustard plaid wool, cut:
❧ 5 of Template A below for Dresden centers
❧ 4 of Template B below for Dresden half-centers

From *each* of the 5" assorted color wool squares, cut:
❧ 4 of Template C below for Dresden petals for a total of 112

From black print, cut:
❧ 5—9" squares for appliqué blocks
❧ 4—8½" squares for non-appliquéd blocks
❧ 2—4" x 24½" side strips for outer border
❧ 2—4" x 31½" top and bottom strips for outer border
❧ 4—2½" strips the width of fabric for binding

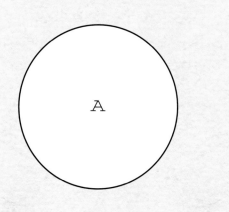
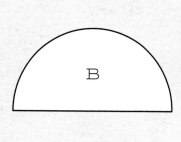
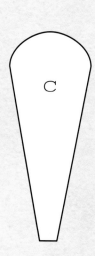

TEMPLATES

# SEWING INSTRUCTIONS

## Quilt Center

1. Fold a 9" black print square in half vertically and finger-press it. Open the fabric up and fold it in half horizontally, then finger-press it.

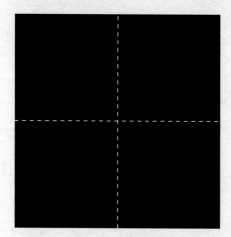

2. Using the finger-pressed lines from the previous step as a guide, lay out 16 Dresden petals to form a circular shape, being careful to leave an approximately 1½"-wide opening in the middle and about ¹⁄₁₆" of space between each Dresden petal so that the thread can easily pass around each shape and lay nice and flat when appliquéing them later.

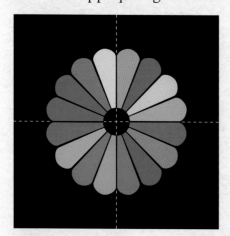

3. Position one dark mustard wool circle in the 1½"-wide space left in the previous step.

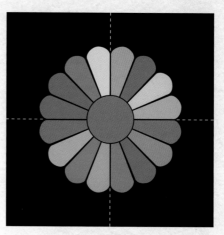

4. When satisfied with placement, affix in place by pressing if using fusible, glue baste or pin if not. This will keep them in position as you sew. Using a blanket stitch, appliqué all the wool pieces to the black print square.

### Blanket Stitch

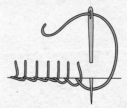

5. Repeat steps 1–4 to create a total of five Dresden Plate blocks.

6. Trim each of the five blocks to measure 8½" square. (The blocks are cut larger originally to accommodate the distortion that can occur during the appliqué process.)

**7.** Lay out the five Dresden Plate blocks and
   4—8½" black print squares into three rows of
   three blocks each. Sew the rows together, then
   join the rows to complete the quilt center.

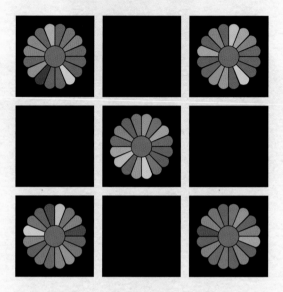
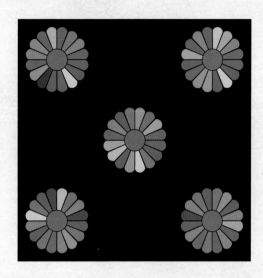

## Outer Border

1. Referring to the quilt assembly diagram on page 71, sew the 2–4" x 24½" black print strips to the sides of the quilt center. Press seams toward the outer border.

2. Referring to the quilt assembly diagram, sew the 2–4" x 31½" black print strips to the top and bottom of the quilt top. Press seams toward the outer border.

3. Referring to the photo on page 66 for placement, lay out eight Dresden petals to create a half Dresden Plate shape in the center of a border strip. Repeat with the remaining three border strips. Then place a mustard wool half-circle in the middle of each half Dresden Plate shape. Affix in place using your chosen method. Using a blanket stitch, appliqué the wool pieces to the four border strips.

### Blanket Stitch

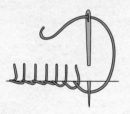

## Finishing the Quilt

Sandwich the quilt top, batting, and backing; baste. Quilt as desired, then bind. Tara used a tan quilting thread that matches the tiny print in the black print. She stitched in-the-ditch around each of the Dresden Plates in the quilt center and around each of the half Dresden Plates in the border. She quilted 7" Dresden Plate designs in the alternating non-appliquéd black blocks. For the border, she used a quilting stencil with a 3"-wide cable design.

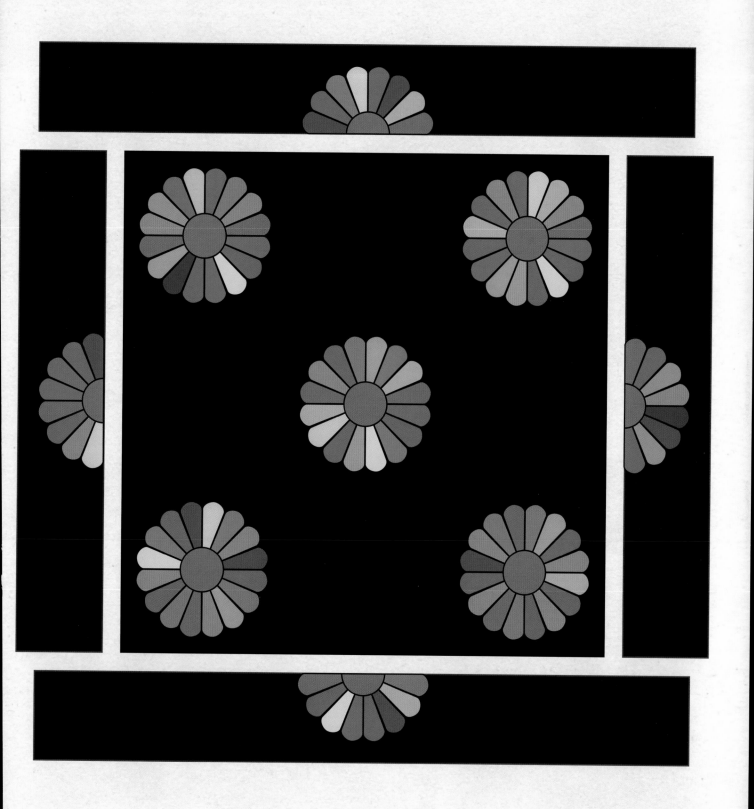

QUILT ASSEMBLY DIAGRAM

# FULL BLOOM

Designed and made by Tara Lynn Darr

Finished size: 29½" x 29½"

*Inspired by my love of Rose of Sharon blocks, I designed this flowery delight. The swags and roses in the outer border add a lovely flourish to the overall design. I had so much fun working on this project that I can definitely see more Rose of Sharon designs in my future!*

## FABRIC REQUIREMENTS

○ 16" x 20" olive green wool for leaves, stems, and border swags

○ 10" square red wool for flower buds

○ 9" x 14" red plaid wool for center block and border flowers

○ 8" square mustard plaid wool for flower centers

○ 1½ yards primitive muslin or other tan mottled cotton for background and binding

○ 36" square fabric of choice for backing

### TARA'S TIPS
Don't be afraid to think outside the box. Your flowers needn't all be red like the featured quilt. Harvest a host of other hues from your wool stash to make a multi-colored bouquet of roses.

## CUTTING INSTRUCTIONS

*If using the fusible web appliqué method, you will need to reverse the templates. For instructions on how to reverse templates, see page 14 in the **Wool Appliqué Basics** section. Labels below correspond with the template labels on pages 77 and 78. Please refer to those before cutting fabrics so you know which piece needs to be cut with what fabric.*

From olive green wool, cut:
- 20 of Template B on page 77 for stems
- 40 of Template C on page 77 for leaves
- 12 of Template G on page 78 for border swag
- 4 of Template H on page 78 for border corner swag

From red plaid wool, cut:
- 21 of Template E on page 77 for block and border flowers

From red wool, cut:
- 20 of Template A on page 77 for flower buds
- 20 of Template D on page 77 for flower buds

From mustard plaid wool, cut:
- 21 of Template F on page 77 for block and border flower centers

From primitive muslin, cut:
- 5—7" squares for appliquéd block backgrounds
- 4—6½" squares for non-appliquéd block backgrounds
- 4—6" x 18½" side strips for outer border
- 2—6" x 29½" top and bottom strips for outer border
- 4—2½" strips the width of fabric for binding

# SEWING INSTRUCTIONS

## Quilt Center

1. Fold a 7" muslin square in half vertically, then finger-press it. Open the fabric up and fold it in half horizontally, then finger-press it.

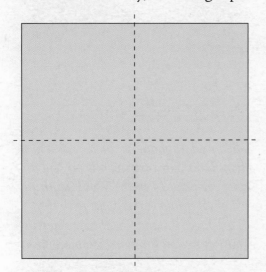

2. Using the finger-pressed lines from the previous step as a guide for placement, lay out the wool appliqué shapes on the muslin background square. Note that the dashed lines in the template on page 77 indicate which pieces are overlapped.

3. When satisfied with placement, affix by pressing if using fusible, glue baste or pin if not. This will keep them in position as you sew. Using a blanket stitch, appliqué the wool pieces to the muslin background square. Using gold thread, stitch three French knots on each of the flower buds. Tara also stitched a few long running stitches in the center of each rosebud with a gold thread.

Blanket Stitch         French Knot

4. Repeat steps 1–3 to create a total of five appliquéd blocks. Then trim the blocks to measure 6½" square. (The blocks are cut larger originally to accommodate the distortion that can occur during the appliqué process.)

5. Referring to the following diagram, lay out the five appliquéd blocks and four 6½" muslin squares into three rows of three blocks each. Sew the rows together, then join the rows to complete the quilt center, which should measure 18½" square.

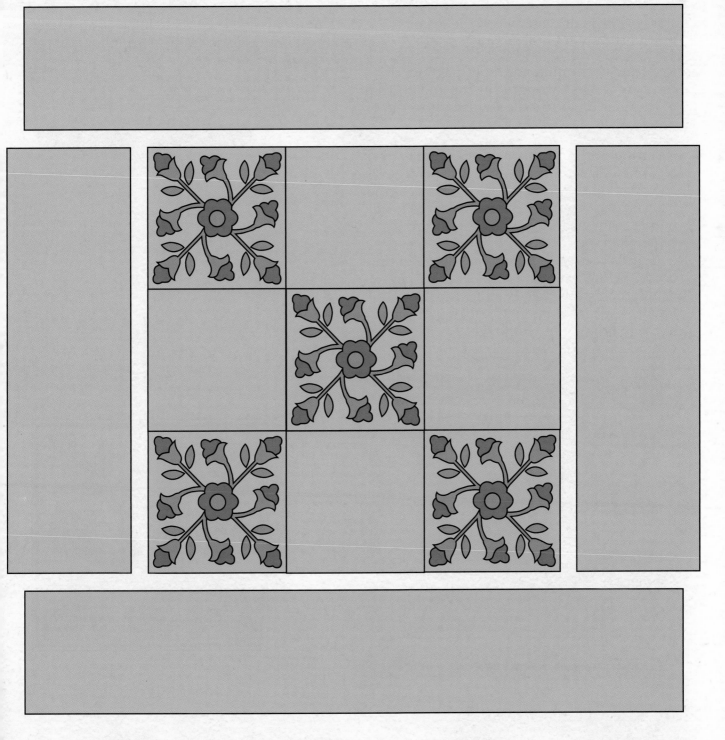

QUILT ASSEMBLY DIAGRAM

## Outer Border

1. Referring to the quilt assembly diagram on page 75, sew the 2–6" x 18½" strips to the sides of the quilt center. Press the seams toward the outer border.

2. Referring to the quilt assembly diagram, sew the 2–6" x 29½" strips to the top and bottom of the quilt top. Press the seams toward the outer border.

3. Referring to the photo on page 72 for placement, lay out the swags, corner swags, and roses on the border strips. Tara places the flowers first, centered ½" away from the inside border seam where it connects to the quilt center. She then arranges the green swags, and tucks their ends under each flower in the border before arranging each of the corner swags, tucking their ends under the flowers. Finally, she places the gold wool flower centers in the middle of the red flowers.

4. When satisfied with placement, affix by pressing if using fusible, glue baste or pin if not. This will keep them in position as you sew. Using a blanket stitch, appliqué all the pieces to the border.

Blanket Stitch

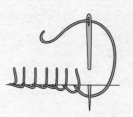

## Finishing the Quilt

Sandwich the quilt top, batting, and backing; baste. Quilt as desired, then bind. Using a thread that matches the background fabric, Tara outline-quilted each of the flowers in the quilt center. In the alternating non-appliquéd blocks, she quilted a 5" flower design. For the border, she quilted a ½" grid on the diagonal to make the swags pop.

TEMPLATES

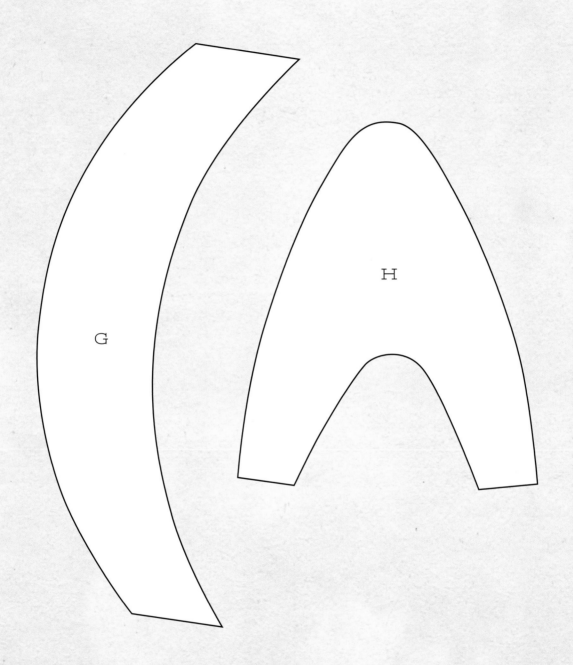

G

H

BORDER TEMPLATES

# RESOURCES

**Hand-dyed wool:**

Blackberry Primitives
1944 High Street
Lincoln, NE 68502
www.blackberryprimitives.com

Primitive Gatherings
850 Racine Street
Menasha, WI 54952
www.primitivegatherings.us

**Non-hand-dyed wool:**

Blackberry Primitives
1944 High Street
Lincoln, NE 68502
www.blackberryprimitives.com

Primitive Gatherings
850 Racine Street
Menasha, WI 54952
www.primitivegatherings.us

Heavens to Betsy
www.heavens-to-betsy.com

The Dorr Mill Store
PO Box 88
Guild, NH 03754
www.dorrmillstore.com

The Wool Connection
1326 Lincoln Ave.
Pompton Lakes, NJ 07442
www.thewoolconnection.com

**Cotton fabric:**

First and foremost, always support your local quilt shop! When I cannot find what I need locally, I go to these three online quilt shops because of the variety of cotton fabrics, fat quarters, and other sized fabric bundles that they carry:

Homestead Hearth (their scrap bags are excellent)
105 North Coal Street
Mexico, MO 65265
www.homesteadhearth.com

The Quilt Merchant
27 West 209 Geneva Road
Winfield, IL 60190
www.thequiltmerchant.com

Primitive Gatherings
850 Racine Street
Menasha, WI 54952
www.primitivegatherings.us

**Thread:**

Primitive Gatherings (sells Valdani thread)
850 Racine Street
Menasha, WI 54952
www.primitivegatherings.us

www.followthatthread.com (sells Aurifil Lana wool thread)

Sue Spargo Folk-art Quilts (sells Tristan wool thread)
3743 Boettler Oak Drive, Suite 2A
Uniontown, OH 44685
www.suespargo.com

# RESOURCES

**Hand-dyed embroidery floss:**

The Gentle Art
P.O. Box 670
New Albany, OH 43054
www.thegentleart.com

Weeks Dye Works
www.weeksdyeworks.com (Click on the
"retailers" link for a list of quilt shops
that carry their thread)

**Scissors:**

Primitive Gatherings (sells Dovo scissors,
which work great on wool and cotton)
850 Racine Street
Menasha, WI 54952
www.primitivegatherings.us

Karen Kay Buckley (sells 4½" and 7½"
Perfect scissors, which work great on
wool and cotton)
1237 Holly Pike
Carlisle, PA 17013
www.karenkaybuckley.com

**Quilting templates:**

The Stencil Company, LLC
217 Altermoor Drive
Natrona Heights, PA 15065
www.quiltingstencils.com

EZ Mark Stencils
13273 County Road 44
Millersburg, IN 46543
574-642-3247

Golden Threads
445 North 700 West
North Salt Lake City, UT 84054
www.goldenthreads.com